HANNA AND THE FLYING CARPET

Heidi Olsson

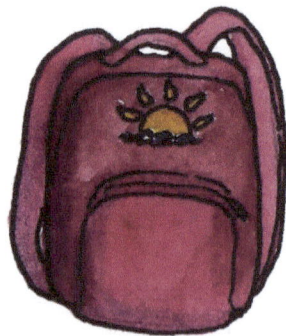

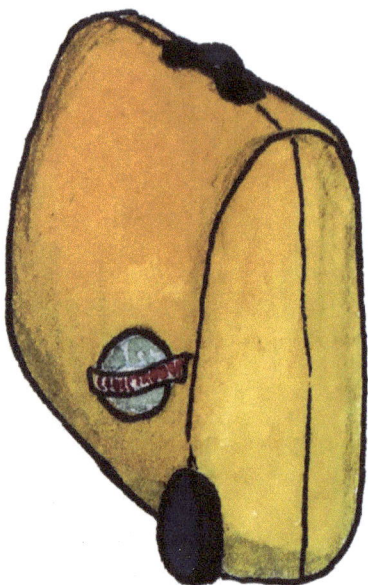

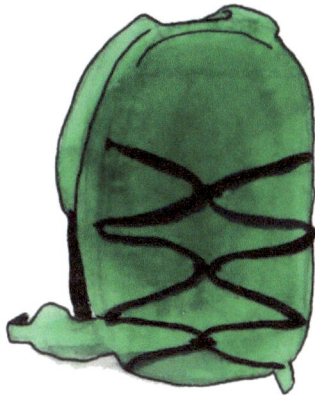

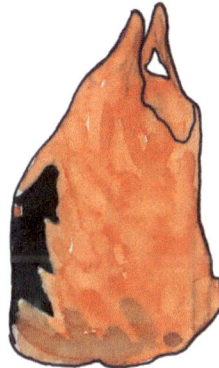

To my family,
and to all kids,
young and older,
who have inspired and helped me.

Show us the world through
your magic eyes!

First published in Great Britain by Springtime Books 2020

Copyright: Heidi Olsson

ISBN: 978-1-9993040-7-2

My name is Hanna. I live in England, but I'm not English. I'm probably Dutch. My parents are from Holland and I lived there before, but my Dutch cousins say that I speak a bit funny. I was born in Kenya. So maybe I'm African?

I've been trying to be English for a year. I like it here. I like my friends, my school, my football training and even my school uniform! Mum says it's time for a new adventure. She looks excited when she says that. Mum loves Africa. I don't want to move to a new place ever again.

I don't want to say goodbye! My friends are planning their summer holidays. I want to go with Sarah to summer camp and with my football team to watch a real game. They know I'll be leaving soon. I wasn't invited to Jenny's birthday party along with the rest of the class.

"Going back to the dangerous snakes, are you?" Patrick said to me yesterday. He's also in my class. I think he was cross with me because I told everyone about the green mamba Mum once beat to death with a spade when I was in Kenya. Not that I remember it, but Dad often talks about it. Patrick had just told us about a viper he had seen in the stone wall behind his house the day before. I guess he thought I was bragging, but what did I know? I've never seen a viper.

I've gone cycling by the canals in Holland, seen large fields of tulips and eaten loads of sandwiches with chocolate sprinkles on them. I have seen Mount Kenya and elephants in the wild, giraffes and even a lion. And in all the places I've lived I have friends. I miss them a lot. I wonder what it would be like to be able to go and see my grandparents for the afternoon whenever I felt like it. What it would feel like to talk to my friends without sounding weird because my accent is all funny. I wish I knew where I belong.

No more goodbyes! Mum tells me to pack my bags, but I'm not going to. They can't pull me out of this room, can they? I'm going to bed now. What's that weird buzzing sound? Who's knocking on the window pane?

Outside my bedroom window, a big bunch of kids swings into view. They wave their arms, suggesting I join them on board.

"Hello! Help! Wow! Where are we going? Who are you guys?" I scream. This is crazier than the craziest thing I've ever read about in a book! Flying carpets belong in stories about Arab boys in ancient times. This one looks a bit more modern though, like a normal carpet from a corridor in an English family home. It has a slightly raised edge on it, which is the only safety equipment I can see. My own home is already far behind us, the wind is strong in my face, but I see someone familiar among all these children.

"Omar! Is that you?"

"Syria next!" says Omar grinning. Omar is a classmate of mine. He seems to be the only one at school apart from me who wasn't born in England. He doesn't say much but he's very good at football. All of a sudden we're arriving at a stone house in Syria! This carpet surely is fast! I can see children leaning out of a window, whispering things loudly in Arabic. They grab Omar and pull him off the carpet.

"Welcome on board, Hanna!" says the boy at the instrument board. Yes, this carpet has a panel full of buttons and levers, and a boy of about my age is actually driving this thing.

"I'm Abdi," he says. "I invented this carpet when I missed my grandmother in Somalia too much. Where would you like to go?"

"I'm thinking about my best friend Caroline in Holland. I really want to be with her again. Utrecht, in Holland, please, Abdi," I answer.

The carpet flies on, leaving and picking up children all over the world. One girl gets to see her brother in Paris and a boy gets to see his best friend in Seoul. A girl gets off at her old boarding school in Calcutta, and a boy gets to see his sisters in Ontario. Even though we have never met before we talk and laugh as if we have known each other all our lives.

It seems we were all born to be travellers. We have made long journeys by plane and by boat. We have eaten new kinds of food, learned new languages and ways of living, and made loads of silly mistakes. We have said goodbye so many times and got to know new friends in new places. Sometimes it has been easy and sometimes we've been teased and bullied. So even though we've lived in such different countries, it's easy to talk with these guys. It's exciting to listen to their stories. And they listen to me without being annoyed.

"Look at this!" says a girl stretching out an arm towards the world beneath our feet. "How lucky we are to get to travel and experience this amazing planet!" Abdi seems to have fun manoeuvring this carpet. One moment we are so high that we can't decide whether we see land or ocean beneath us. The next we are rushing downwards just to find ourselves hovering so close to the surface that we can feel the splashes of the waves. Sometimes we glide through a beautiful valley in the Alps or past a high building in Kuala Lumpur. The next second we fly at such a speed that we see everything around us as foggy lines and only feel quick whiffs of exotic flowers, garbage heaps, spicy food and the salty winds from the sea.

I look down and I see the flat landscape of Holland, the fields criss-crossed with narrow canals and the windmills. Suddenly, there's my own street and we arrive at Caroline's window. Now it's my turn to knock. A confused Caroline leans out to see what is making the sound.

"Hanna?" she asks sleepily. "I must be dreaming," she decides and turns to go back to bed.

I force myself through the window, grab my friend by the shoulder, turn her and kiss her on her cheeks three times, like we learn to do in Holland. She stumbles back in shock.

"See you later!" shouts Abdi happily and flies off to see his grandmother.

Caroline stares at me. She really is waking up slowly. I notice my old cat sleeping soundly on her bed. I run over to him.

"Simba! You're not a kitten anymore!" I laugh at Caroline and bury my face in Simba's fur.

"Is it really you?" asks Caroline. She is starting to smile. I'm trying to keep my voice down but I'm bubbling up with laughter. I use Simba as a silencer, stroking his furry belly. Caroline starts to giggle and hides in her pillow. We can't let her parents hear us. This flying carpet must remain a secret!

"You look just the same!" Caroline says to me. "Even though I haven't seen you for a year!"

"You don't!" I giggle. "Your hair is long and tousled!"
She smiles.

"Look at yourself in the mirror," she says and points at my hair, all roughed up by the wind.

"You want to play?" I ask.

"Of course!" says Caroline and pulls out a box from under her bed. A very dusty box. She opens the lid. There it is – our world that we used to build and play with. "Mum tried to throw it away, but I stopped her."

I pick up an empty chocolate sprinkle box that I painted and made holes in. My old house! And there is our teacher, Karin! We made her from tinfoil, paper and tape, so she has a very shiny dress.

"We have a new teacher now," says Caroline. "She is nice too. She took us to Amsterdam last week."

"How is our secret hiding place?" I ask. "Have you told anyone about it?"

"Of course not! It's secret, remember! And the map is still hidden in the big chestnut tree. But now Anneli and I have a secret club as well. You would have been a member if you were here, of course."

I don't want to talk about that. "We're moving to Tanzania soon," I say, my voice and head drooping sadly at the thought.

"Cool!" says Caroline.

I perk up. Leaving is sad but there are always heaps of great things about a new country too.

"I know! Elephants, lions, white beaches and fresh mangoes. It's a great country! And gorgeous and sunny too," I say, but I still don't want to move!

"I haven't been further away than Germany," says Caroline. "But we'll have a biking holiday this summer. Sleeping in tents and everything."

"Come and visit me, please!" I beg.

Someone is knocking on the window again. It's time to say goodbye. I kiss Simba and Caroline and leap out of the window, onto the carpet.

"Tot ziens, bye bye! See you when I see you!" I say with a smile and hold back the tears. We're off again.

"Did you have a good time?" Abdi asks.

"Yes! Thanks!" I say, though it's reminded me how much I love my old friend and miss her.

"I had a great chat with my granny," says Abdi with a beaming face. I notice he has some rice stuck on his chin. "She always saves some supper for me in case I show up. And it's nice to sit alone with her for a little while when all my new cousins are asleep. It can never be as before though," he says, glancing at me as if he understands that I might burst into tears any minute. "I used to help out with the cows and the everyday chores and listen to the stories in the village, playing with all those friends and everything. At least I can keep seeing my ayooyo."

"You are right," I say. "It was different to just stop by for a visit. But I'm so glad I got to see Caroline again! Thanks, Abdi! Did you know I'll move to Tanzania soon?"

"Wow! Tanzania! That's an amazing country! Let me take you there so you can have a look," says Abdi.

The air gets hotter and damper as we move over the African coastline, scouting out the white beaches of Tanzania, the pineapple plantations and the village women milking their cows in the early morning. As we glide over the Serengeti, I lean out and stroke a giraffe on its head. I suddenly feel happy and adventurous.

We go to collect Omar. We have to tug really hard to get him up on the carpet, away from all those cousins. His eyes are stuck on that stone house until it looks like a little dot, swallowed by a sea of sand. Then he sits down, staring ahead as if someone switched him off.

"How are you?" I ask. "Was it nice to see them again?"
He smiles, still staring ahead.

"It was so nice!" he says. "And they had saved some food for me too! I just wish I could stay there. But of course I can't. And I can't take them with me either. That's the worst part. I don't know when or if I will see them again."

I sit down next to him, but facing the direction we're headed, with my feet dangling over the edge and think about how our life is full of the best highs and the saddest lows too.

There are big differences between Omar's life and mine. His parents didn't go to a new country because they wanted to, but because they had to. They can't go back to their old country. At least not for a long time. We can. Their journey was dangerous. My journeys have been quite safe. But some things are similar.

"We have magic eyes, you and I," I say to him.

He looks confused.

"They have seen a lot, cried a lot, laughed a lot and talked when our mouths haven't known the language. Now they can see past the way people look and find a friend in anyone."

"You're right," says Omar. "It's as if we have invisible spectacles coloured by all the places we have been. It's not important what people look like, what they wear or which language they speak. You can understand each other if you really want to, and then many problems become small. If people knew how wise we are they would make us prime ministers!" We laugh at the thought.

"Look there! England!" I say, and Omar turns to see as we glide closer. "Yes, it's a good place," he says. "I'll play for Manchester United one day!" He smiles cheekily and raises an eyebrow.

"I'm sure they need you," I giggle as he jumps off at his bedroom to get ready for school. "See you later!"

Parents have all kinds of reasons to take their kids across the world. Some, like Omar's, bring their children on a dangerous journey to find a safer and better future for themselves and their children. Others, like mine, want to do some good for others. (I should be proud of them, I guess.)

Some
parents
get jobs in
other countries and
some are just adventurous.
We children just have to
come along for the ride and
I understand now, that it is
a ride, a rollercoaster ride,
exciting and terrifying at the
same time.

"Thank you so much!" I say to Abdi as he drops me off at my bedroom window.

"Who knows, I might pick you up again some time," he says. He waves and flies off.

I look into the mirror. I have dark lines under my eyes. I yawn. I have hardly slept at all, but I feel calm. I'm ready for my next adventure. I'll pack my bag today after school, and I'll start by giving Sarah my football. I sign it with a big black marker pen. Maybe she'll remember me better now? Then I draw my house in England and my new home in Tanzania, an arrow between the two, and write: "Come and visit. It's not that far!"

I promise to share with her how I'm finding life in Tanzania. To describe how the lions' coats shine in the sun, what we learn about at school and whether there's anyone as good as Omar at football. Mum's always telling me that I've got 'magic eyes'. I think our lives are just magic.

It's time for school. Time for those goodbyes and a new adventure.

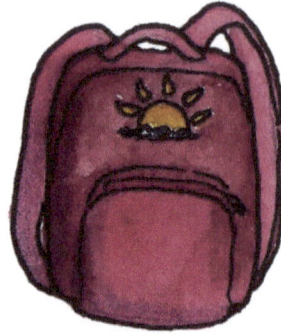

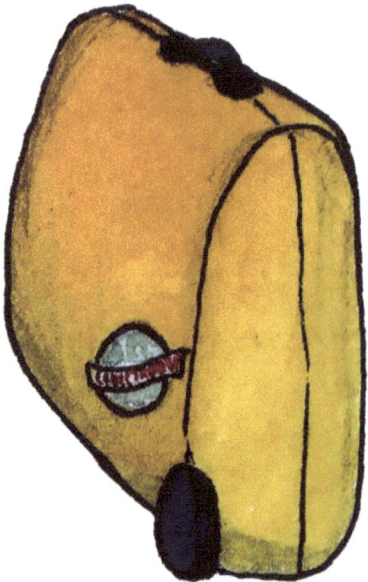

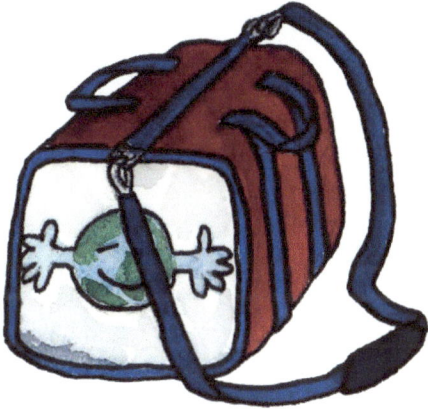

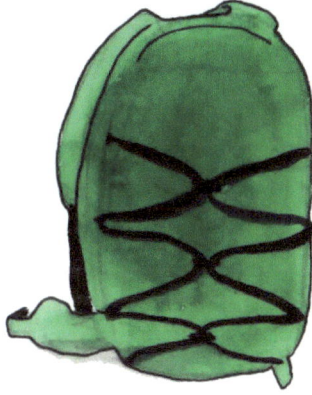

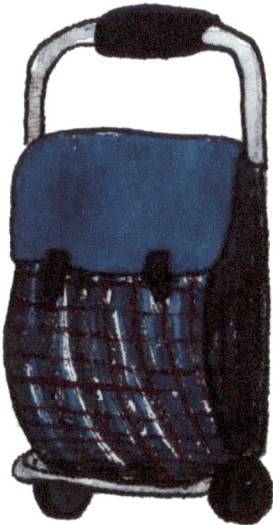

More from Springtime Books and Summertime Publishing

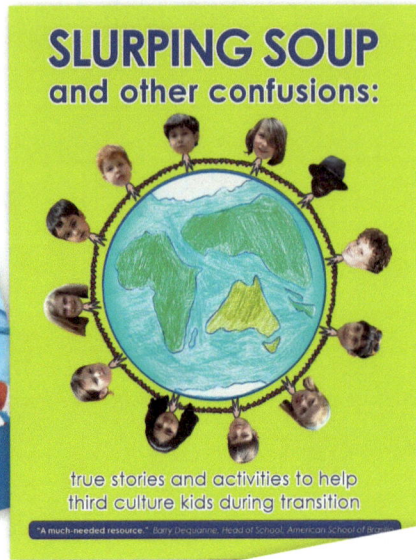

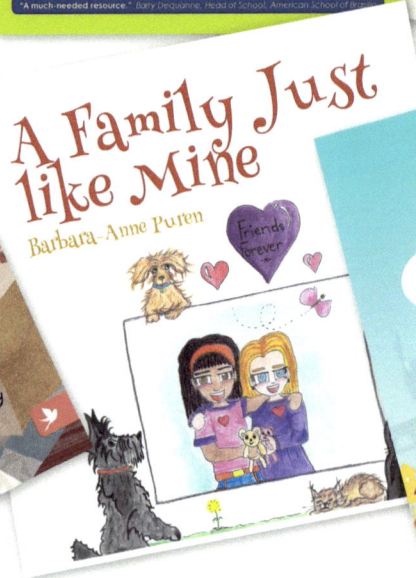

The Mission of Detective Mike Moving Abroad

Susanne T. Costa Eriksson & Anna Sherren (Butterford Ink)

SLURPING SOUP and other confusions:

true stories and activities to help third culture kids during transition

"A much-needed resource." Barry Dequanne, Head of School, American School of Brasilia

my Moving Booklet

We will miss you very much and wish you all the best on your new adventures!

created by Valerie Besanceney

B at Home

Emma Moves Again

By Valerie Besanceney

A Family Just like Mine

Barbara-Anne Puren

Friends forever

I'm moving!

Sara Wallén

www.ingramcontent.com/pod-product-compliance
Lightning Source LLC
Chambersburg PA
CBHW041241020426
42333CB00002B/38

9 781999 304072